WHAT HAVE I EVER LOST BY DYING?

BY ROBERT BLY

Poetry
Silence in the Snowy Fields
The Light Around the Body
Sleepers Joining Hands
Jumping Out of Bed
This Tree Will Be Here for a Thousand Years
The Man in the Black Coat Turns
Loving a Woman in Two Worlds
Selected Poems

Prose Poems
The Morning Glory
This Body Is Made of Camphor and Gopherwood

Prose
The Eight Stages of Translation
A Little Book on the Human Shadow
American Poetry: Wildness and Domesticity
Iron John: A Book About Men
Remembering James Wright

Translations
The Story of Gösta Berling by Selma Lagerlöf
Hunger by Knut Hamsun
Twenty Poems of Georg Trakl
Neruda and Vallejo: Selected Poems
Lorca and Jimenez: Selected Poems
Friends: You Drank Some Darkness:
Three Swedish Poets, Martinson, Ekelöf, and Tranströmer
The Kabir Book: 44 of the Ecstatic Poems of Kabir
Twenty Poems of Rolf Jacobsen
Twenty Poems of Vincente Aleixandre *(with Lewis Hyde)*
Selected Poems of Rainer Maria Rilke
Time Alone: Selected Poems of Antonio Machado
Twenty Poems of Olav H. Hauge
Ten Poems of Francis Ponge Translated by Robert Bly and
Ten Poems of Robert Bly Inspired by the Poems of Francis Ponge

Editor
Leaping Poetry
The Sea and the Honeycomb: 80 Tiny Poems
News of the Universe: Poems of Twofold Consciousness
Forty Poems Touching on Recent American History
A Poetry Reading Against the Vietnam War
The Winged Life: Selected Poems and Prose of Thoreau

Interviews
Talking All Morning: Collected Interviews and Conversations

WHAT HAVE I EVER LOST BY DYING?

COLLECTED PROSE POEMS

BY

ROBERT BLY

HarperCollins*Publishers*

Permission acknowledgments appear on pages xiii–xiv.

HarperCollins books may be purchased for educational,
business, or sales promotional use. For information,
please call or write: Special Markets Department,
HarperCollins Publishers, Inc., 10 East 53rd Street, New
York, NY 10022. Telephone: (212) 207-7528; Fax: (212)
207-7222.

FIRST EDITION

Designed by Fritz Metsch

LIBRARY OF CONGRESS CATALOGING-IN-PUBLICATION DATA
Bly, Robert.
    What have I ever lost by dying? : collected prose
poems / Robert Bly. — 1st ed.
        p.   cm.
ISBN 0-06-016817-X (cloth)
1. Prose poems, American.   I. Title.
PS3552.L9W48   1992
811'.54—dc20   91-50459

92 93 94 95 96 DT/HC 10 9 8 7 6 5 4 3 2 1

For Mary
who brought me a gift

CONTENTS

ACKNOWLEDGMENTS

I am grateful to the editors of the following magazines who published some of these poems: *Kayak, Crazy Horse, Apple, Modern Occasions, Knife River Press, Cafe Solo, The Iowa Review, Hearse, Dragonfly, It, New York Quarterly, Panjandrum, Tennessee Poetry Journal, Tony Petrosky's Broadside Series, Isthmus, New Letters, Chicago Review, Clear Creek, Choice, Peace and Pieces, Sceptre Press, Tempest, UT Review, Field, Sadvipra, Madrona, Poetry, Parabola, Inroads, Germination, Caliban,* and *Ploughshares.*

Twenty of these poems appeared earlier in *The Morning Glory*, published by Kayak Press, copyright © 1969–1970 by Robert Bly. Thanks to George Hitchcock for permission to republish them here. Harper & Row published an enlarged edition of *The Morning Glory* in 1975.

"The Hockey Poem" originally appeared in the *Ohio Review*.

The section called "The Point Reyes Poems" was published earlier by Mudra Press as a pamphlet called "Point Reyes Poems," reprinted later by Floating Island Press. I am grateful to the editors for permission to reprint them here.

"Coming In for Supper" originally appeared in *This Body Is Made of Camphor and Gopherwood*, copyright © 1977 by Robert Bly.

"The Crow's Head," under the title "Solitude of the Two Day Snowstorm," and "Walking Where the Plows Have Been Turning" appeared in *This Tree Will Be Here for a Thousand Years*, copyright © 1979 by Robert Bly.

"Eleven O'Clock at Night," "The Dried Sturgeon," "A Bouquet of Ten Roses," "Visiting Emily Dickinson's Grave with Robert Francis," and "Finding an Old Ant Mansion"

DISAPPOINTMENT AND DESIRE

When I composed the first of these poems, which George Hitchcock published in a collection called *The Morning Glory*, I hoped that a writer could describe an object or a creature without claiming it, without immersing it like a negative in his developing tank of disappointment and desire. I no longer think that is possible.

Our desires and disappointments have such hunger that they pull each sturgeon or hollow tree into themselves. Or it may be that our desires, our aggressions and rages are already inside the sturgeon even before we approach it.

In an object or thing poem, we usually work to keep the imaginative language spare, so that the being does not dissolve into human images; but I have learned also to accept the fantasy that often appears toward the end of the poem. We could say that the complicated soul from which images and language flows is as much nature as the rice grain or the pine cone.

Robert Bly

I lived for hundreds of thousands of years as a mineral,
And then I died and was reborn as a plant.

I lived for hundreds of thousands of years as a plant,
And then I died and was reborn as an animal.

I lived for hundreds of thousands of years as an animal,
And then I died and was reborn as a human being.

What have I ever lost by dying?

Rumi
(version by Robert Bly)

PART 1

THE POINT REYES POEMS

NOVEMBER DAY AT McCLURE'S BEACH

Alone on the jagged rock at the south end of Mc-Clure's Beach. The sky low. The sea grows more and more private, as afternoon goes on; the sky comes down closer; the unobserved water rushes out to the horizon—horses galloping in a mountain valley at night. The waves smash up the rock; I find flags of seaweed high on the worn top, forty feet up, thrown up overnight; separated water still pooled there, like the black ducks that fly desolate, forlorn, and joyful over the seething swells, who never "feel pity for themselves," and "do not lie awake weeping for their sins." In their blood cells the vultures coast with furry necks extended, watching over the desert for signs of life to end. It is not our life we need to weep for. Inside us there is some secret. We are following a narrow ledge around a mountain, we are sailing on skeletal eerie craft over the buoyant ocean.

THE STARFISH

It is low tide. Fog. I have climbed down the cliffs from Pierce Ranch to the tide pools. Now the ecstasy of the low tide, kneeling down, alone. In six inches of clear water I notice a purple starfish—with nineteen arms! It is a delicate purple, the color of old carbon paper, or an attic dress . . . at the webs between the arms sometimes a more intense sunset red glows through. The fingers are relaxed . . . some curled up at the tips . . . with delicate rods . . . apparently globes on top of each, as at world's fairs, waving about. The starfish slowly moves up the groin of the rock . . . then back down . . . many of its arms rolled up now, lazily, like a puppy on its back. One arm is especially active and curves up over its own body as if a dinosaur were looking behind him.

How slowly and evenly it moves! The starfish is a glacier, going sixty miles a year! It moves over the pink rock, by means I cannot see . . . and into marvelously floating delicate brown weeds. It is about the size of the bottom of a pail. When I reach out to it, it tightens and then slowly relaxes. . . . I take an arm and quickly lift. The underside is a pale tan. . . . Gradually, as I watch, thousands of tiny tubes begin rising from all over the underside . . . hundreds in the mouth, hundreds along the nineteen underarms . . . all looking . . . feeling

. . . like a man looking for a woman . . . tiny heads blindly feeling for a rock and finding only air. A purple rim runs along the underside of every arm, with paler tubes. Probably its moving-feet.

I put him back in. He unfolds—I had forgotten how purple he was—and slides down into his rock groin, the snaillike feelers waving as if nothing had happened, and nothing has.

CALM DAY AT DRAKE'S BAY

A sort of roll develops out of the bay, and lays itself all down this long beach. . . . The hiss of the water wall two inches high, coming in, steady as lions, or African grass fires. Two gulls with feet the color of a pumpkin walk together on the sand. A snipe settles down . . . three squawks . . . the gulls agree to chase it away. Then the wave goes out, the waters mingle so beautifully, it is the mingling after death, the silence, the sweep—so swift—over darkening sand. The airplane sweeps low over the African field at night, lost, no tin cans burning; the old woman stomps around her house on a cane, no lamp lit yet . . .

WELCOMING A CHILD IN THE LIMANTOUR DUNES

For Micah

Thinking of a child soon to be born, I hunch down among friendly sand grains. . . . The sand grains love a worried man—they love whatever lives without force, a young girl who looks out over her life, alone, with no map, no horse, a white dress on. The sand grains love whatever is not rushing blindly forward, the mole blinking at the door of his crumbly mole Vatican, and the salmon far out at sea that senses in its gills the Oregon waters crashing down. Something loves even this planet, abandoned here at the edge of the galaxy, and loves this child who floats inside the Pacific of the womb, near the walls, feeling the breakers roaring.

AN EXCURSION ON TOMALES BAY

For Michael and Barbara Whitt

The blue sky suddenly gone—fog. We cut the engine and drift. We glimpse a derrick on shore—it is a bird— a Great Blue Heron! He turns his head and walks away . . . like some old Hittite empire, all the brutality forgotten, only the rare vases left, and the elegant necks of the women. . . .

Heavy bodies float nearby; we drift among them. Whiskered heads peer over at us attentively, like angels called to look at a baby. They have risen from their sea-mangers to peer at us. Their Magi come to them every day . . . and they gaze at the godless in their wooden boat. . . .

Boulders lie piled on the shore . . . no . . . sea lions, hundreds of them! . . . Some on their backs playing. . . . Now the whole shore starts to roll seaward, barking and flapping. . . .

Meanwhile, the whiskered heads have vanished; they are somewhere in the water underneath us. At last one head pops up five feet from the boat, looking neither arrogant nor surprised, but like a billfold found in the water, or a mountain that has been rained on for three weeks . . . and the Great Blue Heron, each wing as long as Holland, flies off, thin as a grassblade in the fog . . .

TWO SOUNDS WHEN WE SIT
BY THE OCEAN

Waves rush up, pause, and drag pebbles back around stones . . . pebbles going out. . . . It is a complicated sound, as of small sticks breaking, or kitchen sounds heard from another house. . . . Then the water draws down farther over the stones always wet. . . . Suddenly the sound of harsh death waves as the ocean water races up the roof of loose stones, leaving a tiny rattling in the throat as it goes out. . . . And the ecstatic brown sand stretched out between stones: the anger of some young women is right.

And always another sound, a heavy underground roaring in my ears from the surf farther out, as if the earth were reverberating under the feet of one dancer. It is a comforting sound, like the note of Paradise carried to the Egyptian sands, and I hear the driftwood far out singing, what has not yet come to the surface to float, years that are still down somewhere below the chest, the long trees that have floated all the way from the Pacific islands. . . . And the donkey the disciples will find standing beside the white wall . . .

THE DEAD SEAL

Walking north toward the point, I come on a dead seal. From a few feet away, he looks like a brown log. The body is on its back, dead only a few hours. I stand and look at him. There's a quiver in the dead flesh: My God, he's still alive. And a shock goes through me, as if a wall of my room had fallen away.

His head is arched back, the small eyes closed; the whiskers sometimes rise and fall. He is dying. This is the oil. Here on its back is the oil that heats our houses so efficiently. Wind blows fine sand back toward the ocean. The flipper near me lies folded over the stomach, looking like an unfinished arm, lightly glazed with sand at the edges. The other flipper lies half underneath. And the seal's skin looks like an old overcoat, scratched here and there—by sharp mussel shells maybe.

I reach out and touch him. Suddenly he rears up, turns over. He gives three cries: Awaark! Awaark! Awaark!—like the cries from Christmas toys. He lunges toward me; I am terrified and leap back, though I know there can be no teeth in that jaw. He starts flopping toward the sea. But he falls over, on his face. He does not want to go back to the sea. He looks up at the sky, and he looks like an old lady who has lost her hair. He puts his chin back down on the sand, rearranges his flippers, and waits for me to go. I go.

The next day I go back to say goodbye. He's dead now. But he's not. He's a quarter mile farther up the shore. Today he is thinner, squatting on his stomach, head out. The ribs show more: each vertebra on the back under the coat is visible, shiny. He breathes in and out.

A wave comes in, touches his nose. He turns and looks at me—the eyes slanted; the crown of his head looks like a boy's leather jacket bending over some bicycle bars. He is taking a long time to die. The whiskers white as porcupine quills, the forehead slopes. . . . Goodbye, brother, die in the sound of the waves. Forgive us if we have killed you. Long live your race, your inner-tube race, so uncomfortable on land, so comfortable in the ocean. Be comfortable in death then, when the sand will be out of your nostrils, and you can swim in long loops through the pure death, ducking under as assassinations break above you. You don't want to be touched by me. I climb the cliff and go home the other way.

FINDING A SALAMANDER
ON INVERNESS RIDGE

Walking. Afternoon. The war still going on, I stoop down to pick up a salamander. He is halfway across the mossy forest path. He is dark brown, fantastically cold in my hand. This one is new to me—the upper part of his eyeball light green . . . strange bullfrog eyes. The belly is brilliant orange, color of airplane gasoline on fire; the back is a heavy-duty rubber black, with goose pimples from permanent cold. I make a kind of pulpit of my left hand, and turn him gently upright; his head and front legs look out at me, as his hands rest on my crossing thumb joint. Warmed, he grows lively, pulls himself out, and falls to earth, where he raises his chin defiantly. I pick him up again. But he is patient. I hold him again between thumb and forefinger for many minutes, and his front paws hold on to my thumb resignedly—perhaps I could hold him so for hours. Perhaps he could be held gently this way for days until he died, the green eyes still opening and closing. When I turn my wrist over, I see the long orange-black tail hanging down into the cathedral of the open palm, circling back and forth, rolling and unrolling like a snake. It hangs down like a rudder on some immensely long boat, a rudder that the men and women on board looking over the handrail do not see.

TRESPASSING
ON THE PIERCE RANCH

I walk toward Tomales Point over soaked and lonely hills—a wild cat runs away from his inspection of a wet gopher's hole as I come near. Wind off the sea. A few sheep, some cows with large udders high above the ocean.

These cliffs are the first land the amazed traveler saw when he looking over the rail suddenly came on a continent . . . in the middle of the endless ocean.

Glancing east, I see the three-quarters moon moving in broad daylight, pale and urgent, through the sky, freeing itself from the clouds. It is a sturdy eye-traveler, sailing eerily forward, orphaned, bold and alone. Formed long ago, it has parted from the earth as my moon from myself.

Part of me then must be sailing steadily through clouds, and the rest of me is down here, among these soaked and lonely hills. These hills rise toward the coastal range and again toward the Rockies where they thicken at last into Nebraska, and into the plateau that holds up the heavy pueblos, Taos, San Isidro, Isleta.

The ten-year-old boys of Taos run fast, their heels hitting the earth-drum; the old men strike the boys lightly with twigs as they run past. When the boys arrive at the playa, they see the old men have lifted up a cottonwood trunk, and tied a sacrificed sheep to the very top.

OCTOBER AT PIERCE RANCH

I scramble down a ravine along walls eaten away by the rain. Seasound. It is low tide. Seagulls trailed by their shadows stroll among scarfs of seaweed on long willful legs; their bodies float like notes never written down.

I walk down the sandy valley arms swinging, and I feel excitement, ready to leap into the air, chew the sand.

But that other one in me feels not excited, but exultant, for he hears sounds not coming from the blood, purer, deeper, wilder.

PART 2

FAMILY POEMS

AUGUST RAIN

.

After a month and a half without rain, at last, in late August, darkness comes at three in the afternoon. A cheerful thunder begins, and then the rain. I set a glass out on a table to measure the rain and, suddenly buoyant and affectionate, go indoors to find my children. They are upstairs, playing quietly alone in their doll-filled rooms, hanging pictures, thoughtfully moving "the small things that make them happy" from one side of the room to another. I feel triumphant, without need of money, far from the grave. I walk over the grass, watching the soaked chairs, and the cooled towels, and sit down on my stoop, pulling a chair out with me. The rain deepens. It rolls off the porch roof, making a great puddle near me. The bubbles slide toward the puddle edge, become crowded, and disappear. The black earth turns blacker; it absorbs the rain needles without a sound. The sky is low, everything silent, as when parents are angry. . . . What has failed and been forgiven —the leaves from last year, under the porch, retreat farther into the shadow; they give off a faint hum, as of bird's eggs, or the tail of a dog.

The older we get the more we fail, but the more we fail the more we feel a part of the dead straw of the universe, the corner of a barn with cowdung twenty years old, the chair fallen back on its head in a deserted farmhouse, the belt left hanging over the chairback after the bachelor has died in the ambulance on the way to the city. These objects belong to us; they ride us as the child holds on to the dog's fur; they appear in our dreams; they approach nearer and nearer, coming in slowly from the wainscoting. They make our trunks heavy, accumulating between trips. These objects lie against the ship's side, and will nudge the hole open that lets the water in at last.

COMING IN FOR SUPPER

It is lovely to follow paths in the snow made by human feet. The paths wind gaily around the ends of drifts, they rise and fall. How amazed I am, after working hard in the afternoon, that when I sit down at the table, with my elbows touching the elbows of my children, so much love flows out and around in circles. . . . The children have been working on a play.

Each child flares up as a small fire in the woods. . . . Biddy chortles over her new hair, curled for the first time last night, over her new joke song.

> *Yankee Doodle went to town,*
> *riding on a turtle,*
> *turned the corner just in time*
> *to see a lady's girdle. . . .*

Mary knows the inscription she wants on her coffin if she dies young, and says it:

> *Where the bee sucks there suck I*
> *In a cowslip's bell I lie. . . .*

She is obstinate and light at the same time, a heron who flies pulling long legs behind, or balances unsteadily on a stump, aware of all the small birds at the edge of the forest, where it is shadowy . . . longing to capture the horse with only one hair from its mane. . . .

Biddy can pick herself up and run over the muddy river bottom without sinking in; she already knows all about holding, and kisses each grownup carefully before going to bed; at the table she faces you laughing, bending over slightly toward you, like a tree bent in wind, protective of this old shed she is leaning over. . . .

And all the books around on the walls are feathers in a great feather bed, they weigh hardly anything! Only the encyclopedias, left lying on the floor near the chair, contain the heaviness of the three-million-year-old life of the oyster-shell breakers, those long dusks—they were a thousand years long then—that fell over the valley from the cave mouth (where we sit). . . . The inventions found, then lost again . . . the last man killed by flu who knew how to weave a pot of river clay the way the wasps do. . . . Now he is dead and only the wasps know in the long river-mud grief. The marmoset curls its toes once more around the slippery branch, remembering the furry chest of its mother, long since sunk into a hole that appeared in the afternoon.

Dinner is finished, and the children pass out invitations composed with felt pens.

You are invited to
"The Thwarting of Captain Alphonse"

PRINCESS GARDINER:	Mary Bly
CAPTAIN ALPHONSE:	Wesley Ray
AUNT AUGUST:	Biddy Bly
RAILWAY TRACK:	Noah Bly
TRAIN:	Sam Ray

Costumes and Sets by Mary Bly and Wesley Ray
Free Will Offering Accepted

CLIMBING UP MOUNT VISION
WITH MY LITTLE BOY

We started up. All the way he held my hand. Sometimes he falls back to bend over a banana slug, then senses how lonely the slug is, and comes running back. He never complained, and we went straight up. How much I love being with him! How much I love to feel his small leafy hand curl around my finger. He holds on, and we are flying through a cloud. On top we hunker down beneath some bushes to get out of the wind, while the girls go off to play, and he tells me the story of the little boy who wouldn't cut off his hair and give it to a witch, and so she changed him into a hollow log! A boy and girl came along, and stepped on the log —and the log said, "Oww!" They put their feet on it again, and the log said, "Oww!" Then they looked inside and saw a boy's jacket sticking out. A little boy was in there! "I can't come out, I've been changed into a hollow log." That's the end, he said.

Then I remembered a bit more—the boy and the girl went to a wise man . . . he corrected me, "It was a wise woman, Daddy," . . . and said, "How can we get him changed back into a little boy?" She said, "Here is a pearl. If a crow asks you for it, give it to him." So they went along. Pretty soon a crow came and said, "Can I have the buttons on your shirt?" The boy said, "Yes." Then the crow said, "Can I have that pearl in your shirt pocket?" "Yes." Then the crow flew up and dropped some moss down the witch's chimney. The chimney got full, the witch started to cough. The crow dropped in some more moss. Then she had to open the door, and run outside! Then the crow took an oyster, a big one, from the Johnson Oyster Company, and flew high into the air, and dropped it right on the witch's head. And that was the end of her. And then the boy was changed back again into a little boy.

The land on top is bare, sweeping, forbidding—so unlike a little boy's mind. I asked him what he liked best about the whole walk. He said it was Bethany (an eight-year-old friend of Mary's) going peepee in her pants while hiding.

SITTING ON SOME ROCKS
IN SHAW COVE

I sit in a cliff hollow, surrounded by fossils and furry shells. The sea breathes and breathes under the new moon. Suddenly it rises, hurrying into the long crevices in the rock shelves, it rises like a woman's belly as if nine months has passed in a second; rising like the milk to the tiny veins, it overflows like a snake going over a low wall.

I have the sensation that half an inch under my skin there are nomad bands, stringy-legged men with fire-sticks and wide-eyed babies. The rocks with their backs turned to me have something spiritual in them. On these rocks I am not afraid of death; death is like the sound of the motor in an airplane as we fly, the sound so steady and comforting. And I still haven't found the woman I loved in some former life—how could I, when I have loved only twice on this rock, though twice in the moon, and three times in the rising water. My daughters in my mind's eye run toward me, laughing, arms in the air. A bird with long wings comes flying toward me in the dusk, pumping just over the darkening waves. He has flown around the whole planet; it has taken him centuries. He returns to me the lean-legged runner laughing as he runs through the stringy grasses, and gives back to me my buttons, and the soft sleeves of my sweater.

THE CROW'S HEAD

Supper time. I leave my cabin and start toward the house. Something blowing among the tree trunks. . . . My frail impulses go to shelter behind thin trees, or sail with the wind. A day of solitude over . . . the time when after long hours alone, I sit with my children, and feel them near. . . . At what I want to do I fail fifty times a day, and am confused. At last I go to bed.

I wake before dawn hearing strong wind around the north bedroom windows. On the way to the cabin, I see dust of snow lying on yesterday's ice. All morning snow falls.

By noon I give up working, and lie listening to the wind that rises and falls. Sometimes it makes the sound of a woman's skirt pulled swiftly along the floor. . . . At other times it gives a slow growl without anger like the word *Enoch*. . . .

I go to the window. The crow's head I found by the bridge this summer, and brought home, stands on the window sash. Feathers edge its Roman beak. It is fierce, decisive, the one black thing among all this white.

FINDING AN OLD ANT MANSION

The rubbing of the sleeping bag on my ear made me dream a rattlesnake was biting me. I was alone, waking the first morning in the North. I got up, the sky clouded, the floor cold. I dressed and walked out toward the pasture. And how good the unevenness of the pasture feels under tennis shoes! The earth gives little rolls and humps ahead of us. . . .

The earth never lies flat, but is always thinking, it finds a new feeling and curls over it, rising to bury a toad or a great man, it accounts for a fallen meteor, or stones rising from two hundred feet down, giving a little jump for Satan, and a roll near it for Calvin. . . . I turn and cut through a strip of cleared woods; only the hardwoods are still standing. As I come out into the pasture again, I notice something lying on the ground.

It's about two feet long. It is a wood-chunk, but it has open places in it, caves chewed out by something. The bark has fallen off, that was the roof. . . . I lift it up and carry it home kitty-corner over the field.

When I set it on my desk, it stands. The base is an inch or two of solid wood, only a bit eaten by the acids that lie in pastures. The top four or five inches is also solid, a sort of forehead.

In between the forehead and the base there are sixteen floors eaten out by ants. The floors flung out from the central core are light brown, the color of workmen's benches, or old eating tables in Norwegian farmhouses. The open places in between are cave-dark, the heavy brown of barn stalls in November dusk, the dark the cow puts her head into at the bottom of mangers. . . . A little light comes in from the sides, as when a woman at forty suddenly sees what her mother's silences as she washed clothes meant, and which are the windows in the side of her life she has not yet opened.

And these open places are where the ant legions labored—the antlered layers awakening, antennae brush the sandy roof ceilings, low and lanterned with the bull-heat of their love—and the lively almsgivers go forth, over the polished threshold passed by thousands of pintaillike feet, with their electricity for all the day packed into their solid-state joints and carapaces. Caravans go out, climbing, gelid with the confidence of landowners; and soon they are at work, right here, making delicate balconies where their eggs can pass their childhood in embroidered chambers; and the infant ants awaken to old father-worked halls, uncle-loved boards, walls that hold the sighs of the pasture, the moos of confused cows, sound of oak leaves in November, sound of grasshoppers passing overhead, some car motors from the road, held in the sane wood, given shape by Osiris' love.

Now it seems to be a completed soul home. These balconies are good places for souls to sit, in the half-dark. If I put it on our altar, souls of the dead in my family can come and sit now, I will keep this place for them. The souls of the dead are no bigger than a grain of wheat when they come, yet they too like to have their backs protected from the wind of nothing, the wind of Descartes, and of all who grew thin in maternal deprivation. Vigleik can come here, with his lame knee, pinned in 1922 under a tree he himself felled, rolling cigarettes with affectionate fingers, patient and protective. And my brother can sit here if he can find the time, he will bring his friend if he comes; my grandmother will come here surely, sometimes, with the ship she gave me. This balcony is like her kitchen to the southwest, its cobstove full of heating caves; and Olai with his favorite horse and buggy, horsehide robe over his knees, ready to start for town, with his mustache; the dead of the Civil War, Thomas Nelson, fat as a berry, supported by his daughters: and others I will not name I would like to come. I will set out a drop of water and a grain of rye for them. What the ants have worked out is a place for our destiny, for we too labor, and no one sees our labor. My father's labor who sees? It is in a pasture somewhere not yet found by a walker. Meanwhile it is still open to the rains and snows. All labor still unfound is open to the rains and snows, who are themselves ants, who go into dark crevices and live.

CHRISTMAS EVE SERVICE
AT MIDNIGHT AT ST. MICHAEL'S

For Father Richter

A cold night; the sidewalk we walk on icy; the dark surrounds the frail wood houses that were so recently trees. We left my father's house an hour before midnight, carrying boxes of gifts out to the car. My brother, who had been killed six months before, was absent. We had wept sitting near the decorated tree. Now I see the angel on the right of St. Michael's altar kneeling on one knee, a hand pressed to his chin. The long-needled Christmas pine, who is the being inside us who is green both summer and winter, is hung with red ribbons of triumph. And it is hung with thirty golden balls, each ball representing a separate planet on which that eternal one has found a home. Outdoors the snow labors its old Manichean labors to keep the father and his animals in melancholy. We sing. At midnight the priest walks down one or two steps, finds the infant Christ, and puts him into the cradle beneath the altar, where the horses and the sheep have been waiting.

Just after midnight, he turns to face the congregation, lifts up the dry wafer, and breaks it—a clear and terrifying sound. He holds up the two halves . . . frightening . . . like so many acts, it is permanent. With his arms spread, the cross clear on his white chasuble, he tells us that Christ intended to leave his body behind. It is confusing . . . we want to take our bodies with us when we die. I see waters dark and lifting near flights of stairs, waters lifting and torn, over which the invisible birds drift like husks over November roads. . . . The cups are put down. The ocean has been stirred and calmed. A large man is flying over the water with wings spread, a wound on his chest.

IN PRAISE OF A GRAIN OF RICE

The rice grain has the shape of a loaf, and it is translucent almost, for four fifths of its length. It seems to contain hope, and to be made of hard light. Lying in my palm, it is almost weightless, a fragment of the pre-mammal world, without blood, but with spirit, a dry vegetable spirit that dances in the sieve, whose sound awakens Dionysius sleeping in some cradle.

The first-quarter moon, sharp in the morning sky, looks hard as well. The moon solidified long ago. Sunlight leaves it but does not enter it; and its stains represent the dark side of the light, the boy put in prison for picking up sticks on the Sabbath.

So, at night, somber images flow across the face of the grain of rice; monks weep, and even the grain looks inward at its own vegetable inheritance.

When I lift it to my tongue, and let it be, the tongue understands ancestral bodies that do not dissolve when the oil of suffering flows over them. And so of our children—it must be that they will not dissolve. Each child is a grain of engendered light, threshed from thousands of feathery plants, and did not come from us, from father and mother, at all.

Their souls and ours come and go, obedient to some other moon. The feathery plants wave all night in the rice paddies, and the moon silently lifts the ocean waters in and out over the granite threshold.

ELEVEN O'CLOCK AT NIGHT

I lie alone in my bed; cooking and stories are over at last, and some peace comes. And what did I do today? I wrote down some thoughts on sacrifice that other people had, but couldn't relate them to my own life. I brought my daughter to the bus—on the way to Minneapolis for a haircut—and I waited twenty minutes with her in the somnolent hotel lobby. I wanted the mail to bring some praise for my ego to eat, and was disappointed. I added up my bank balance, and found only $65, when I need over a thousand to pay the bills for this month alone. So this is how my life is passing before the grave?

The walnut of my brain glows. I feel it irradiate the skull. I am aware of the consciousness I have, and I mourn the consciousness I do not have.

Stubborn things lie and stand around me—the walls, a bookcase with its few books, the footboard of the bed, my shoes that lie against the blanket tentatively, as if they were animals sitting at table, my stomach with its curved demand. I see the bedside lamp, and the thumb of my right hand, the pen my fingers hold so trustingly. There is no way to escape from these. Many times in poems I have escaped—from myself. I sit for hours and at last see a pinhole in the top of the pumpkin, and I slip out that pinhole, gone! The genie expands and is gone; no one can get him back in the bottle again; he is hovering over a car cemetery somewhere.

Now more and more I long for what I cannot escape from. The sun shines on the side of the house across the street. Eternity is near, but it is not *here*. My shoes, my thumbs, my stomach, remain inside the room, and for that there is no solution. Consciousness comes so slowly, half our life passes, we eat and talk asleep— and for that there is no solution. Since Pythagoras died the world has gone down a certain path, and I cannot change that. Someone not in my family invented the microscope, and Western eyes grew the intense will to pierce down through its darkening tunnel. Air itself is willing without pay to lift the 707's wing; and for that there is no solution. Pistons and rings have appeared in the world; valves usher gas vapor in and out of the theater box ten times a second; and for that there is no solution. Something besides my will loves the woman I love. I love my children, though I did not know them before they came. I change every day. For the winter dark of late December there is no solution.

A VISIT TO THE OLD PEOPLE'S HOME

We drive to see my parents, through prairie where the reddish color has come again to the sloughs. The tall ash trees around the Lutheran Home are bare; a few yellow leaves lie on the big wooden swings so seldom used.

Entering their room, I feel a shock looking at my mother's face for she has had a stroke, her first, a week ago. The right side of her mouth and eye are drawn down. I sit down next to my father's bed, and Ruth begins massaging Alice's feet, for the shoes with pointed toes she wore for so many years have deformed her toes on the right foot.

My father tells me quietly that the stroke happened to Alice inside during the night, and only gradually happened to her face. He noticed it first at lunch when he sat across from her. He then called his daughter-in-law, who told the nurses. My mother says to the room all at once: "What happened to me?" Jacob says—I don't know why—"Nothing happened to you." "Yes, it did," she says, "I had a stroke." "She doesn't think it's fair that it should happen to her," Jacob says.

And what do I do? It's not I who massage my mother's feet. I am angry that her beauty has been taken away from me; it seems to lessen me, and I am afraid to look at her. How little pity I have for her.

We need to close up the lake cabin for the winter, and we drive north for hours through the wet October farms, some new snow falling from abruptly darkening clouds. Clouds vanish, replaced by blue cold sky.

When we arrive at the lake, it is nearly dark. I walk into the water with my shoes off, and, starting at the end of the dock, remove the bolts that hold the dock surface to the standing pipes. I work toward shore, handing the bolts to Ruth, while the wooden dock sections, freed, rest on the ledges attached to the pipes. As I take out the final bolt, I say, "Here's another bolt for you." As she reaches for the bolt, she steps on the dock section, now utterly unattached, and it abruptly pivots, slants downward, and she drops with it into four or five inches of chill water. Why didn't I mention that the section was no longer fastened?

She dries her feet. We carry up the pieces, lay the dock in sections on the cold wet grass. Then we finish the rest of the tasks, shutting off the water, and so on. I push the warped windows shut from the outside, and she latches them on the inside. As we prepare to leave, we both step out on the stoop. The front door lock snaps shut, with the keys to the house and the car still inside.

PART 3

OBJECTS
AND CREATURES
GLANCED AT
BRIEFLY

A POTATO

The potato reminds one of an alert desert stone. And it belongs to a race that writes novels of inspired defeat. The potato does not move on its own, and yet there is some motion in its shape, as if a whirlwind paused, then turned into potato flesh when a ghost spit at it. The skin mottles in parts; potato cities are scattered here and there over the planet. In some places papery flakes lift off, light as fog that lifts from early morning lakes.

Despite all the eyes, we know that little light gets through. Whoever goes inside will find a weighty, meaty thing, both damp and cheerful, obsessive as a bear that keeps swimming across the same river.

When we open our mouth and bite into the raw flesh, both tongue and teeth pause astonished, as a bicyclist leans forward when the wind falls. The teeth say: "I could never have imagined it." The tongue says: "I thought from the cover that there would be a lot of plot . . ."

AN OYSTER

The oyster looks impenetrable and thuggy, and is the size of a baby mountain lion's paw. Its surface is flaky, breaking off, crazily staked with little abdominal errors. There are waves here, as on gypsy skirts—concealing what?

Hands, as they move to open it, feel grainy, about to violate a privacy. Small flakes of subtle calcium fall away; they are the grief and surprise that come away from lips closed so long. We have to call for a knife, which is the gift of those who lived before us, a strong knife, the end simpleminded but without Puritanism; it arranges its hard-ended molecules so as to recapture the past, gallop up the valley, return the dead to their former lives.

The oyster body wets the tip of the nose as one tries to gulp it up . . . the lips feel satisfied, as if they deserve what they have received.

And when we see the two empty shells, we feel it is right to praise the naked life. The shells are ready now to be thrown away into gardens, or thrown back into the ocean, as simple plates of desire.

A CATERPILLAR
MY DAUGHTER BROUGHT TO ME

For Mary

She comes and lays him carefully in my hand—a caterpillar! A yellow stripe along his back, and how hairy! Hairs wave like triumphal plumes as he walks.

Just behind his head, a black something slants back, like a crime, a black memory leaning toward the past.

He is not as beautiful as my three-year-old daughter thinks: the hair falling over his mouth cannot completely hide his face—two sloping foreheads with an eye between, and an obstinate jaw, made for eating through sleeping things without pain of conscience. . . .

He rears on my hand, looking for another world.

LOOKING AT A DEAD WREN
IN MY HAND

Forgive the hours spent listening to radios, and the words of gratitude I did not say to teachers. I love your tiny ricelike legs, that are bars of music played in an empty church, and the feminine tail, where no worms of Empire have ever slept, and the intense yellow chest that makes tears come. Your tail feathers open like a picket fence, and your bill is brown, with the sorrow of a rabbi whose daughter has married an athlete. The black spot on your head is your own mourning cap.

THE PORCUPINE IN THE WIND

In half-light, I make out a shape near a tree trunk—a half-grown porcupine! He hurries clumsily—like a steam shovel—up the tree. Six feet up, he decides he has gone far enough; and he waits, occasionally looking at me over a half-turned shoulder. Stepping up, I look into his eye, which is black, with little spontaneity, above an expressionless nose. He knows little about climbing, and his claws keep slipping on the gray poplar bark. His body apparently feels no excitement anyway to be climbing higher, toward the immaterial sky: he can't remember any stories he has heard.

Sun already down. The white needle-fur stands out, something pre-Roman, next to the elegant bark. As I listen I become aware of a third thing, still older. It is the wind through miles of leafless forest.

A BIRD'S NEST MADE OF
WHITE REED FIBER

The nest is white as the foam thrown up when the sea hits rocks! It is translucent as those cloudy transoms above Victorian doors, and swirled as the hair of those intense nurses, gray and tangled after long nights in the Crimean wards. It is something made and then forgotten, like our own lives that we will entirely forget in the grave, when we are floating, nearing the shore where we will be reborn, ecstatic and black.

A CATERPILLAR

Lifting my coffee cup, I notice a caterpillar crawling over my sheet of ten-cent airmail stamps. The head is black as a Chinese box. Nine soft accordions follow it around, with a waving motion like a flabby mountain. Skinny brushes used to clean pop bottles rise up from some of its shoulders. As I pick up the sheet of stamps, the caterpillar advances around and around the edge, and I see his feet: three pairs under the head, four spongelike pairs under the middle body, and two final pairs at the tip, pink as a puppy's hind legs. As he walks, he rears, six pairs of legs off the stamp, waving around in the air! One of the sponge pairs, and the last two tail pairs, the reserve feet, hold on anxiously. It is the first of September. The leaf shadows are less ferocious on the notebook cover. A man accepts his failures more easily—or perhaps summer's insanity is gone? A man notices ordinary earth, scorned in July, with affection, as he settles down to his daily work, to use stamps.

AN OCTOPUS

I hear a ticking on the Pacific stones. A white shape is moving in the furry air of the seacoast. The moon narrow, the sea quiet. He comes close; a long time the stick ticks on over the rock faces. Is it a postal employee saddened by the sleet? It comes nearer. I talk. The shape talks, it is a Japanese man carrying a spear and a heavy-bellied little bag. The spear has a hook on the end. What are you looking for, clams? No! Octopus!

Did you get any? I found three. He sits down. I get up and walk over. May I see them? He opens the plastic bag. I turn on the flashlight. Something wet, fantastic, womblike, horse intestine–like. May I take hold of one? His voice smiles. Why not? I reach in. Dry things stick to my hands, like burrs from burdocks, compelling, pleading, dry, poor, in debt. You boil them, then sauté them. I look and cannot find the eyes. He is a cook. He ate them in Japan.

So the octopus is gone now from the mussel-ridden shelf with the low roof, the pool where he waited under the thin moon, but the sea never came back, no one came home, the door never opened. Now he is taken away in the plastic bag, not understood, illiterate.

A GODWIT

Shorebirds occupy a patch of sand near the ocean. Eighteen or twenty godwits work, driving their long frail beaks into sand recently made slate-colored by the falling tide. A dozen turn their backs to the surf and walk inland, striding on legs purposeful and thin. Their abrupt walk integrates motions that seem contrary to us, as when a jerking branch somehow joins the flow of the river. Now the flock feeds again—each lifts the head briefly to swallow, then drives the bill back into sand; when the bill is down, the whole body shakes, the tail feathers bob up and down. Each time the head lifts, the eyes are black, calm, alert, keeping watch. . . .

One godwit, not as plump as the others, stands balanced on one leg, the other drawn up. My breath pauses as I notice that the foot is missing, and in fact the whole leg below the knee is gone. When he hops, his isolated knee bends like the other one; his single foot kicks a little sand away with each step. Feeding and hopping, he comes up near one of the plump ones, and with a swift motion, perfectly in rhythm, bites him in the ass. He then hops out of the flock and feeds alone.

It took me so long to notice that one bird was not a real member of the flock; the flock moves continually, striding or flying. Sometimes the flock strides away and leaves him; at other times feeds around him. The flock rises once more and flies toward the sea where the packed sand shines. The bird with one leg rises with them, but turns in the air, his long wings tipping among the winds, and lands at his old place to feed alone.

A ROCK CRAB

A rock crab sits heavily on a mess of greenish-brown seaweed; ocean water still gleams on his shell. He is matter, substantiality, *accidentia*, a heavy downpouring of primitive light. The mottled shapes on the top suggest desert forts.

A hand reaches out and turns him over, and we see the underside of the rock crab, fierce like the underside of the Sahara. The six claws folded over the stomach are joined segments of what has to be done, hard bits of necessity. The will is strong, living without mother or father, bony, unsentimental, even on the upper legs that slope like arms. Inside the girlish arms there is cold and muscular flesh, still visionary, washed at night when seawater carries its moony splashings through the claw tunnel.

If we get down on our knees and inhale the odor, we feel suddenly vulnerable, as when we recall at noon a detail from last night's dream. Something has put our face close to the truth, to the bony teeth of the ocean.

A BOX TURTLE

The orange stripes on his head shoot forward into the future. The turtle's slim head stretches out, and it pushes with all its might, caught now on the edge of my palm. The claws—five on the front, four in back—are curiously long and elegant, cold, curved, pale, like a lieutenant's sword. The yellow stripes on the neck and head remind you of racing cars.

The bottom plate is a pale, washed-out rose color from being dragged over the world. The imagination is simplified there, without too much passion, business-like—like the underside of a space ship.

WALKING WHERE THE PLOWS
HAVE BEEN TURNING

"The most beautiful music
of all is the music of what happens." —OLD IRISH TALE

For Gioia Timpanelli

Some intensity of the body came to me at five in the morning. I woke up, I saw the east pale with its excited brood, I slipped from bed, and out the back door, onto the sleek and resigned cottonwood leaves. The horses have gotten out, and are eating in the ditch. . . . I walk down the road toward the west.

I notice a pebble on the road, then a corn ear lying in the ditchgrass, then the earthbridge into the cornfield. I walk on it to the backland where the plows turn, the tractor tires have married it, they love it more than the rest, cozy with bare dirt, the downturned face of the plow that looked at it each round . . .

In the risen sun the earth provides a cornhusk in one place, a cottonwood tree in another, for no apparent reason. A branch has dropped onto the fence wire; there are eternities near, the body free of its exasperations, ready to see what will happen. There is a humming in my body, it is jealous of no one.

The cricket lays its wings one over the other, a faint whispery sound rises up to its head . . . which it hears . . . and disregards . . . listening for the next sound . . .

THE HOCKEY POEM

DULUTH, MINNESOTA

For Bill Duffy

◆ 1 ◆

The Goalie

The Boston College team has gold helmets, under which the long black hair of the Roman centurion curls out. . . . And they begin. How weird the goalies look with their African masks! The goalie is so lonely anyway, guarding a basket with nothing in it, his wide lower legs wide as ducks'. . . . No matter what gift he is given, he always rejects it. . . . He has a number like 1, a name like Mrazek, sometimes wobbling on his legs waiting for the puck, or curling up like a baby in the womb to hold it, staying a second too long on the ice.

The goalie has gone out to mid-ice, and now he sails sadly back to his own box, slowly; he looks prehistoric with his rhinoceros legs; he looks as if he's going to become extinct, and he's just taking his time. . . .

When the players are at the other end, he begins sadly sweeping the ice in front of his house; he is the old witch in the woods, waiting for the children to come home.

◆ 2 ◆

The Attack

They all come hurrying back toward us, suddenly, knees dipping like oil wells; they rush toward us wildly, fins waving, they are pike swimming toward us, their

50

gill fins expanding like the breasts of opera singers; no, they are twelve hands practicing penmanship on the same piece of paper. . . . They flee down the court toward us like birds, swirling two and two, hawks hurrying for the mouse, hurrying down wind valleys, swirling back and forth like amoebae on the pale slide, as they sail in the absolute freedom of water and the body, untroubled by the troubled mind, only the body, with wings as if there were no grave, no gravity, only the birds sailing over the cottage far in the deep woods. . . .

Now the goalie is desperate . . . he looks wildly over his left shoulder, rushing toward the other side of his cave, like a mother hawk whose chicks are being taken by two snakes. . . . Suddenly he flops on the ice like a man trying to cover a whole double bed. He has the puck. He stands up, turns to his right, and drops it on the ice at the right moment; he saves it for one of his children, a mother hen picking up a seed and then dropping it. . . .

But the men are all too clumsy, they can't keep track of the puck . . . no, it is the *puck*, the puck is too fast, too fast for human beings, it humiliates them constantly. The players are like country boys at the fair watching the con man— The puck always turns up under the wrong walnut shell. . . .

They come down ice again, one man guiding the puck this time . . . and Ledingham comes down beautifully, like the canoe through white water, or the lover going upstream, every stroke right, like the stallion galloping up the valley surrounded by his mares and colts, how beautiful, like the body and soul crossing in a poem. . . .

◆ 3 ◆
The Fight

The player in position pauses, aims, pauses, cracks his stick on the ice, and a cry as the puck goes in! The goalie stands up disgusted, and throws the puck out. . . .

The player with a broken stick hovers near the cage. When the play shifts, he skates over to his locked-in teammates, who look like a nest of bristling owls, owl babies, and they hold out a stick to him. . . .

Then the players crash together, their hockey sticks raised like lobster claws. They fight with slow motions, as if undersea . . . they are fighting over some woman back in the motel, but like lobsters they forget what they're battling for; the clack of the armor plate distracts them, and they feel a pure rage.

Or a fighter sails over to the penalty box, where ten-year-old boys wait to sit with the criminal, who is their hero. . . . They know society is wrong, the wardens are wrong, the judges hate individuality. . . .

◆ 4 ◆
The Goalie

And this man with his peaked mask, with slits, how fantastic he is, like a white insect who has given up on evolution in this life; his family hopes to evolve after death, in the grave. He is ominous as a Dark Ages knight . . . the Black Prince. His enemies defeated him in the day, but every one of them died in their beds that night. . . . At his father's funeral, he carried his own head under his arm.

He is the old woman in the shoe, whose house is

never clean, no matter what she does. Perhaps this goalie is not a man at all, but a woman, all women; in her cage everything disappears in the end; we all long for it. All these movements on the ice will end, the seats will come down, the stadium walls bare. . . . This goalie with his mask is a woman weeping over the children of men, that are cut down like grass, gulls that stand with cold feet on the ice. . . . And at the end, she is still waiting, brushing away before the leaves, waiting for the new children developed by speed, by war . . .

PART 4

LOVE POEMS

MORNING BY THE LAKE

For Jim and Sue

Wind blows, and lake water breaks over the bare rocks no one loves. I walk about on bare feet an inch off the ground, and feel the longing to kneel down, to put my knees against the earth. Some thing in me flies out over the water like fragments of lightning, or a beam broken up into sparks.

All at once I understand the Virgin and her candles, and I love the great gray body of the whale rolling in the sea, with his sides glistening, and I understand why my hair is up near the clouds.

That understander in me longs for a room with stone walls, deep bays, and morning sunlight, where a woman with shining arms is sitting.

STANDING UNDER A CHERRY TREE
AT NIGHT

Cherry boughs in blossom sway in the night wind, resembling conductors' hands that follow the note just about to come. The clumps of blossoms bend, forgive, and return petals to the earth.

And we who are married sway like these boughs, as if in heavy canyons, moving upstream against the tiny cedar twigs being turned over and over in the cloudy spring river coming down.

I climbed down today from St. David's Head to the black mussels, and after walking miles along the rocky beach have climbed the cliffs to this friend's orchard. Now it is nearly midnight, and I am a human being standing in the dark looking at the cherry branches above him swaying against the night sky not far from the sea.

A BOUQUET OF TEN ROSES

The roses lift from the green strawberrylike leaves, their edges slightly notched, for the rose is also the plum, the apple, the strawberry, and the cherry. Petals are reddish-orange, the color of a robin's breast if it were silk. I look down into the face of one rose: deep down inside there are somber shades, what Tom Thumb experienced so low under chairs, in the carpet-darkness . . . those growing swirls of gathering shadows, which eyes up near lamps do not see. It is the calm fierceness in the aborigine's eye as he holds his spear polished by his own palm. These inviting lamblike falmers are also the moist curtains on the part of the woman she cannot see; and the cloud that opens, swarming and parting for Adonis. . . . It is an opening seen by no one, only experienced later as rain. And the rose is also the skin petals around the man's stalk, the soft umber folds that enclose so much longing; and the tip shows violet, blind, longing for company, knowing already of an intimacy the thunderstorm keeps as its secret, understood by the folds of purple curtains, whose edges drag the floor.

And in the center of the nine roses, whose doors are opening, there is one darker rose on a taller stem. It is the rose of the tumbling waters, of the strumming at night, the color of the Ethiopian tumblers who put their heads below their feet on the Egyptian waterfront, wheeling all over the shore. . . . This rose is the man sacrificed yesterday, the silent one wounded under the oak, the man whose dark foot needs to be healed. He experiences the clumsy feeling that can only weep. It is the girl who has gone down to the world below, disobeying her mother, in order to bring calm to the house, traveling alone . . . and the rose windows of Chartres, the umber moss on the stag's antlers . . .

GRASS FROM TWO YEARS

When I write poems, I need to be near grass that no one else sees, as in this spot, where I sit for an hour under the cottonwood. The long grass has fallen over until it flows. Whatever I am . . . if the great hawks come to look for me, I will be here in this grass. Knobby twigs have dropped on it. The summer's still green crosses some dry grass beneath, like the hair of the very old, that we stroke in the morning.

And how beautiful this ring of dry grass is, pale and tan, that curves around the half-buried branch—the grass flows over it, and is pale, gone, ascended, no longer selfish, no longer centered on its mouth; it is centered now on the God "of distance and of absence." Its pale blades lie near each other, circling the dry stick. It is a stick that the rain did not care for, and has ignored, as it fell into the night on men holding horses in the courtyard; and the sunlight was glad that the branch could be ignored, and did not ask to be loved— so I have loved you—and the branch and the grass lie here deserted, a part of the wild things of the world, noticed only for a moment by a heavy, nervous man who sits near them, and feels that he has at this moment more joy than anyone alive.

THE COUPLE I DO NOT KNOW
SITTING BY THE SHORE
NEAR CARMEL

A woman chats with a man while they sit on a rock above the sea. I surmise that the man is talking about things perceptible to him; but the woman, as she looks out over the sea, knows that a child is approaching. The sun setting behind Point Lobos makes the water surface gleamy, glowing, rolling; the sea lifts on invisible shoulders, silvery, dangerous, tense, furred with seaweed hide, silent, luminous in its golden light-patches, glorified by all that is gone and absent; and the persistent waters push on through and above the offshore rocks, and more behind, more rising.

The granite of the peninsula shelters this cave from the wider sea, which is whale-ridden, only lightly touched by human beings, too mad for the small boater.

The shrewd one in her is helpless to predict who will be born; the being who usually knows knows nothing; all she knows is that the ocean labors to give birth to the night. The walled garden, under whose earth the true bride, after being killed and cut to pieces, will be buried, labors to give birth to the laughing boy, who will one day skip and laugh among the white stones.

And so the man and woman go on chatting as they look out over the ocean. An otter appears, holding a shell on its chest. Violet streams drift down from the full moon.

PART 5

LOOKING FOR
THE RAT'S HOLE

WARNING TO THE READER

Sometimes farm granaries become especially beautiful when all the oats or wheat are gone, and wind has swept the rough floor clean. Standing inside, we see around us, coming in through the cracks between shrunken wall boards, bands or strips of sunlight. So in a poem about imprisonment, one sees a little light.

But how many birds have died trapped in these granaries. The bird, seeing the bands of light, flutters up the walls and falls back again and again. The way out is where the rats enter and leave; but the rat's hole is low to the floor. Writers, be careful then by showing the sunlight on the walls not to promise the anxious and panicky blackbirds a way out!

I say to the reader, beware. Readers who love poems of light may sit hunched in the corner with nothing in their gizzards for four days, light failing, the eyes glazed. . . . They may end as a mound of feathers and a skull on the open boardwood floor . . .

THE TOUCH
OF THE MOTH'S ANTENNA

Below a stone bridge made of fitted rock on which I sit at Glacier National Park, the snow melt water flows by. When I feel something brush my knuckle, I open my eyes. It is a moth.

The moth's skinny legs are crooked as cottonwood twigs. Its wings are tan, the color of a pitchfork handle that shows through the hay, but in parts deeper brown, the color of chopped tobacco, loved by old men. Circles that look like eyes decorate the wings. And its hairs flow around the tubular body as currents of air flow around a fuselage.

I call over to a friend to look, but when her shadow falls on my hands the moth lifts, is gone. Abashed, I resume my waiting. After a moment the moth descends from over my shoulder, and settles down on the same knuckle. The moth leans its antennae over . . . and the long searcher touches the skin. The skin feels each touch for long afterward. His wings are serrated and have battlements.

Last night I dreamt that some friends and I were driving and a Plymouth pulled up close behind. "Oh, oh, we have visitors," I said. The Plymouth pulled past, and it was not the police, but a speeding car that a moment later turned and crashed into the trees. The people in that car sat upright shocked. Three pas-

sengers in the backseat—not dead but motionless—
faced toward the road already passed. All three had
masks on.

A HOLLOW TREE

I bend over an old hollow cottonwood stump, still standing, waist high, and look inside. Early spring. Its Siamese temple walls are all brown and ancient. The walls have been worked on by the intricate ones. Inside the hollow walls there is privacy and secrecy, dim light. And yet some creature has died here.

On the temple floor feathers, gray feathers, many of them with a fluted white tip. Many feathers. In the silence many feathers.

OPENING THE DOOR OF A BARN
I THOUGHT WAS EMPTY
ON NEW YEAR'S EVE

Having walked over fields made white with new snow, I open the double barn doors and go in. Sounds of breathing! Thirty steers are wandering around, the old partitions gone. Creatures heavy, shaggy, slowly moving in the dying light. Bodies with no St. Teresas look straight at me. The floor is cheerful with clean straw. Snow gleams in the feeding lot through the other door. The bony legs of the steers look frail in the pale light from the snow, like uncles who live in the city.

Dust and cobwebs thicken the windowpanes. The dog stands up on his hind legs to look over the worn wooden gate. Large shoulders watch him, and he suddenly puts his paws down, frightened. After a while, he puts them up again. A steer's head swings to look at him; it stares for three or four minutes, unable to get a clear picture from the instinct reservoir—then bolts.

But the steer's enemies are asleep; the barn is asleep. These steers do not demand eternal life; they ask only to eat the crushed corn and the hay, coarse as rivers, and sometimes feel an affection run down along the heavy nerves. Each of them has the wonder and bewilderment of the large animal, a body with a lamp lit inside fluttering on a windy night.

DAWN IN THRESHING TIME

The three-bottom plow is standing in the corner of a stubble field. The flax straw lies exhausted on the ground.

The dawning sun slants over the wet pigeon grass, so that the slope of highway ditches is like a face awakening from sleep.

The oat stubble is shiny. Swaths still to be combined are wet. The farmer puts on his jacket and goes out. Every morning as he gets up after thirty he puts on besides his jacket the knowledge that he is not strong enough to die, which he first felt deep in his wooden cradle at threshing time.

THE DRIED STURGEON

Climbing down from the bridge at Rock Island, Illinois, I cross some tracks. It is October. Westward the black railway bridge makes short hops across the river. The riverbank is confused with drifted leaves, chill, the sand cold in late October.

A dried-out fish. . . . It is a sturgeon. . . . It is stiff, all its sudden motion gone. I pick it up . . . its speckled nose-bone leads back to the eyesocket . . . and behind that there is a dark hole where the gills once were.

So the darkness enters just behind the head. It is the darkness under the bunched leaves, the soothing darkness ten feet down in sand. The pine tree standing by the roadhouse holds the whole human night in one needle, just as this opening holds the sweet dark of the hunchback's dreams, where he is straight and whole again, and the earth is flat and crooked. A virgin brings out four black stones for him from beneath her cloak.

Behind the gill opening the scales go on toward the tail. The scales are dry, swift, organized, tubular, straight and humorless as railway schedules, the big clamp of the boxcar, tapering into sleek womanly death.

FROST ON THE WINDOWPANE

Frost is glittery, excited, like so many things laid down silently in the night, with no one watching. Through the two lower panes the watcher can dimly see the three trunks of the maple, sober as Europe. The frost wavers, it hurries over the world, it is like the body that lies in the coffin, and the next moment has disappeared! The mind through its skin picks up the radio signals of death, reminders of the molecules flying all about the universe . . . the icy disembarking, chill fingertips, tulips at head and foot.

I look at the upper panes and see more complicated roads . . . ribbons thrown down on the road . . .

VISITING EMILY DICKINSON'S GRAVE
WITH ROBERT FRANCIS

A black iron fence closes the graves in, its ovals delicate as wine stems. They resemble those chapel windows on the main Aran island, made narrow in the fourth century so that not too much rain would drive in. . . . It is April, clear and dry. Curls of grass rise around the nearby gravestones.

The Dickinson house is not far off. She arrived here one day, at fifty-five, Robert says, carried over the lots between by six Irish laboring men, when her brother refused to trust her body to a carriage. The coffin was darkened with violets and pine boughs, as she covered the immense distance between the solid Dickinson house and this plot. . . .

The distance is immense, the distances through which Satan and his helpers rose and fell, oh vast areas, the distances between stars, between the first time love is felt in the sleeves of the dress, and the death of the person who was in that room . . . the distance between the feet and head as you lie down, the distance between the mother and father, through which we pass reluctantly.

My family addresses "an Eclipse every morning, which they call their 'Father.' " Each of us crosses that distance at night, arriving out of sleep on hands and knees, astonished we see a hump in the ground where we thought a chapel would be. And we clamber out of sleep, holding on to it with our hands . . .

"DEATH COULD COME!"

For Susan Mathews Allard and Her Double Bass

The musician's fingers do not hurry at all as they climb up the Jacob's Ladder of her bass. They are not accomplishing tasks laid down by others, but have agreed to luminous labors suggested—by whom? The fingers go higher. The Cantata says: "Death is not far off . . . Death could come!" Men's and women's voices all around cry out: "It is the ancient law!" Now we sense the odor of roots, of partridge berries, masses of leaves that give up their lives without complaining.

Her fingers appear from the house of the hand-back, as if the hand were a being in itself, with its own slow joys, and its own cottage where it lives, sleeping long on winter nights.

Now the musician's fingers run up the mountain path, they are goats that do a firm dance, one foot down, then the other, many fields and mountain paths with goats on them leaping. . . . And we, who listen, cross a mountain at dusk, we walk a long time through the moor in the dark, at last we see a hut with one lamp lit . . .

AN ANT HILL

Ants working have heaped up this earth hill over-night, and each particle is a stomach traveler that has traveled all the way through Egypt. The travelers now lie crowded together in their humility.

In the center of that heap a hole goes straight down, where humans cannot follow, into the earth. It is surely the hole in the tip of the penis; and also the circular trapdoor in the kitchen floor that opens to the cellar. The Japanese story says that if a woman drops a pan-cake, and then climbs down through the hole to retrieve it, she will meet the green and yellow giants, and will have to cook for them for five years.

This hole then must be death, even though we know the ants did not fabricate death. They made the hole in order to see the light. As I watch, three ants rise, one after the other, and scramble up the crater sides. They move with jerky, electrical motions, fierce, intent on their task.

Last night in my dream several flying saucers ap-peared in the western sky to my mother and me. . . . And later, when they landed near where we stood, I opened a small vein or artery in my finger, so as to mingle my blood with the pale green blood of a plant. When a son is born, the mother is always present. Death then is something that we and our mother must experience together. She gives the son a magic apple; it falls and the son gets down on his knees to look for it; on my knees now, I can no longer see the three ants. They will go over the wide earth and return to this black hole, as to a friend's house.

THE SLATE JUNCO

Alerted by a thump, I go out and close my hand over a gray and white bird that clings to a porch screen wet with October rain. When I carry him in, closed in my left hand, his dark brownish-black eyeballs, over which the lid skims, glow; and one can see a delicate embroidery of feathery islands at the bottom edge. How large, sensuous, and Italian—Florentine—are his tender, alert, impatient, brave, I-may-soon-die eyes.

In the dark fuzz where the bill joins the body we glimpse the power of a being with arrows who arrives from far down in the earth; so this bird is connected not only to air, but to some rooted selfishness in the earth. The bill has the clarity of a three-word question. His bill tip is browner than the rest of the bill, as if it were a stovefront darkened by its own appetite.

Stretching out one wing, I feel delight in the translucent, balanced, disciplined, airy, meditative rows of feathers, each slate-gray with white on the edge nearest the body.

What can one say of this wind animal, so hot in the hand, made so much for the air, the grass, the day, the place where God kills or not? "I shall set off for somewhere; I shall make the reckless choice."

When he turns his head to me, I am looking at a merciless fighter; it is a shock to the part of us that believes that every animal or bird has a gentle lesson to teach us. As I carry him to the door, he is clearly an engine of war, the tree defended, intruders driven away, the beak tip sinking in . . .

THE STUMP

The stump we almost walked past is easily over-looked. But it is vivid when noticed, and resembles an elephant's leg with the body shot off. The short walls still left, their bark loosened here and there by rain, show a wood sleek and silvery, which feels rough to the fingers, uneven as weeks of hospital introspection. It's clear that the big saw did not sever all; and spires stand on its low tower, resembling broken vows. Ivy has crept in; and fallen green needles make the low tower seem gay.

Above the stump other trees go on growing, expand-ing into the air. Vines climb trunks toward light. But there is something in life that doesn't know how to climb; it is sure everything around it that could help it to go upward is dead, or unreliable. I drop my eyes, and walk on with the others to the Fort.

THE BLACK CRAB-DEMON

The ocean swirls up over the searock. It falls back, returns, and rushes over a whirlhole the shape of a galaxy. A black crab climbs up the searock sideways, like a demon listening in Aramaic.

All at once, I am not married; I have no parents; I wave my black claws and hurry over the rock. I hold fast to the bottom; no night-mother can pry me loose; I am alone inside myself; I love whatever is like me. I am glad no seabeast comes to eat me; I withdraw into the rock caverns and return; I hurry through the womb-systems at night.

Last night in my dream a man I did not know whispered in my ear that he was disappointed with me, and that I had lost his friendship. . . . How often have I awakened with a heavy chest, and yet my life does not change.

RENDEZVOUS
AT AN ABANDONED FARM

As we walk out at dawn we can still see the remains of the path the cows have beaten into the weedy earth, and the 75-by-40-foot barn that the farmer inherited and, as Thoreau said, "pushed before him all his life." The barn is used now only for storing hay, the buildings rented out. The barn resembles some African trading post, abandoned when the secrets the Europeans hid caught up with them, and no one could give a "simple and sincere account of his own life."

The Germans and Norwegians who opened this land broke into the earth, ignoring the mother-love of the Sioux. The immigrants have sunk back now into their family Bibles; the great hinges have closed on them, and they sleep a coarse sleep—not forgiven. They know they have done wrong, and they go over and over the harness-hours, trying to see how they threw on the harness, how they happened to buckle things in the wrong order. And the souls of the immigrant women float crippled through the hay loft; the bodies are lacking an arm or foot; the missing parts have been sent to someone as a message, like those hands sent back by kidnappers in the Middle Ages.

It is early dawn. Sunlight bounces from the roofs of the two cars that have brought us. Something is over, has finished here, and there is no comfort, there is no good thing to say.

A PIECE OF LICHEN

This piece of dried lichen was clinging to a rockside in Maine, and I had to bend over, crouching on my knees, reach down over the side of the rock, to get it. It has the consistency of black Chilean deserts seen from the air.

The lichen piece looks like an ox-skin blown about in a dark Thor storm, flopping across the roads near Las Vegas, turning over and over, frightening rabbits and foxes as it rolls. Its edges turn up or under.

It's clear that something is falling out of this chalice now, as if its dried womb cannot contain what it once contained. Something is falling out as if the black one has made a move, as if the dry one will appear, has appeared, and we are in danger of being rolled over by black dryness—invisible in the dry black nights.

The lichen came away easily, was not deeply attached. When we turn it over, we know what it's like to have only enough water to carry you through half of the year.

When the thief who has stolen the blanket arrives back home, he throws the stolen blanket down in a corner of his room. If he folds the blanket, who is there to unfold it?

THE CICADA HUSK

The cicada's husk remains attached to the lower side of a log, the underpinning of a lake cabin. It hangs by its feet-cases. The head-husk, from which the head has already pulled away, amounts to a curious box, with bent turrets and double forehead, the consistency of rice paper; it is frail as those shrimp sheets that curl as they fall into boiling oil.

From the underside of its torso, the first pair of absent legs sets out. The two sections of each absent leg are about an inch long, dry as a wheat stalk, thinned out by delicate terror. And there are more.

But the abdomen-husk—how much one grieves the abdomen with all its vitals and eggs. The lower body shell is made of seven paper lanterns, or overlapping siding on an air house. The empty shell reminds one of those white Japanese paper lanterns that rich parents who want their children to leave hang in the trees for the garden party, so that the children will admire the grandeur of the world.

THE FOG HORNS AT PORT TOWNSEND

The fog horn lasts about five seconds, and then there is a pause. We listen in silence, such waiting silence, the silence when the guests are about to arrive. The fog horn comes again. It says that the world will be born once more, surely it will. And its sound is the color of a brown dog, that lies for a long time before the fire.

The silence goes on a while . . . then a fainter horn farther off . . . another silence . . . then a third still farther away. . . . Then waiting again. The big horn comes. It says that a child has gotten lost on the mountain. Its sound has deep ocean loneliness in it, the long waves far at sea that no hulls pass over, and the moment at dawn when a whole city of sunlight rises up out of the ocean, and the moment at dusk when the saddened village, silent and surly, sinks with its golden roofs down.

There is a child lost on the mountain. It started down the wrong slope of the mountain, and that led it farther away from the others, even though they too were descending. Now the parents have not slept for days. How do they know that the searchers will not go home this morning and drive the jeeps back down the logging roads? "It's no use; we covered the whole area." And if the child is found after having been away so long, who will keep it from going out again? And whose plate will it take?

85

THE FLOUNDER

The coarse grainy skin of the flounder makes one think of remarks made too coarsely, and too quickly. The color is the grayish pale brown of wolf paws. Its petulant, rubbery mouth widens gradually, and the flesh actually is an extension or widening of the mouth. The shape becomes a thick triangle; part way up, the fins continue in thought, in architectural fantasy, what the flesh itself decided not to do. Then at the upper peak, the fins begin to slope off, and by diminishing, make a second triangle sliding away toward the tail; and the tail too has its fin, a sort of afterthought.

It took some violence to get those eyes twisted around to one side—probably the sort of violence each family knows about. Whatever it was, the flounder ended floating along the ocean bottom, white side down, hoping not to be seen from above. The underside does not see the sun; it takes on the paleness of the cutworm, of the upper arms of women who always wear sleeved dresses.

It must be then that half of me stands here on shore, with my long line and casting rod, and the other half is down there, so that what stands above remains attached to what floats down there.

If Joseph had turned into a fish, and Egypt were a great river, then wouldn't Joseph, after he had fled from the Plantation Manager's wife, slipping away, naked, heading for the water, have glided about the legs of the thin cattle soon to rise from the river? He would swim slowly, as those fish whose long black feelers touch the muddy boulders. And if he became a man again, and slipped back into bed, would he be the brother on shore or the brother under the water?

DEFEATING AN ORANGE

The orange's hide is soft and grainy; and it has two navels, as if it were born once into this world, and once into the next. When my mouth opens to bite it, the teeth lose their hold and slide, and we feel abashed, as if a gate were left open and a horse had gotten loose.

The brain turns the orange over to the ten clever ones. The thumbnail enters first, and the nine friends hover around, offering to help. The orange skin now reveals its frightened white underside, as when citizens on the border lift their faces as the tanks approach. The right hand lifts a large flake to the lips; the teeth take it and the lips feel a sting for long afterward. So whoever dominates another has to put up with slightly numb lips. Fingers continue the job on their own, and soon the inner orange lies in the palm, looking scared and naked.

What to do? The thumbs meet while the other eight hold it tight, and after a joint effort the orange falls apart, and the fingertips feel the wet of victory. The hand that holds the half orange inherits the mouth's instinctive longing; and modesty suggests the best solution, to swallow the naked thing. Soon the half orange disappears, and the hand hovers, naked itself, wet, caught in the act, not sure what to do. . . . Perhaps pray or reach down toward the kitchen table for the other half.

THE MUSHROOM

This white mushroom comes up through the duffy lith on a granite cliff, in a crack that ice has widened. The most delicate light tan, it has the texture of a rubber ball left in the sun too long. To the fingers it feels a little like the tough heel of a foot.

One split has gone deep into it, dividing it into two half-spheres, and through the cut one can peek inside, where the flesh is white and gently naive.

The mushroom has a traveler's face. We know there are men and women in Old People's Homes whose souls prepare now for a trip, which will also be a marriage. There must be travelers all around supporting us whom we do not recognize. This granite cliff also travels. Do we know more about our wife's journey or our dearest friends' than the journey of this rock? Can we be sure which traveler will arrive first, or when the wedding will be? Everything is passing away except the day of this wedding.

A CHUNK OF AMETHYST

Held up to the windowlight the amethyst has elegant corridors, that give and take light. The discipline of its many planes suggests that there is no use in trying to live forever. Its exterior is jagged, but in the inner house all is in order. Its corridors become ledges, solidified thoughts that pass each other.

This chunk of amethyst is a cool thing, hard as a dragon's tongue. The sleeping times of the whole human race lie hidden there. When the fingers fold the chunk into the palm, the palm hears organ music, the low notes that make the sins of the whole congregation resonate, and catches the criminal five miles away with a tinge of doubt.

With all its planes, it turns four or five faces toward us at once, and four or five meanings enter the mind. The exhilaration we felt as children returns. . . . We feel the wind on the face as we go downhill, the sled's speed increasing . . .